Crazy for Rivers

ALSO BY BILL BARICH

Laughing in the Hills

Traveling Light

Hard to Be Good

Hat Creek and the McCloud (limited edition)

Big Dreams: Into the Heart of California

Carson Valley

BILL BARICH

WITHDRAWN

Crazy for
Rivers

THE LYONS PRESS

Printed in the United States of America

10 9 8 7 6 5 4 3 2

Design and composition by Wilsted & Taylor Publishing Services

Library of Congress Cataloging-in-Publication Data
Barich, Bill.
      Crazy for rivers/Bill Barich.
         p. cm.
         1. Trout fishing—Anecdotes. 2. Fly fishing—Anecdotes.
    3. Rivers—Anecdotes. 4. Barich, Bill. I. Title.
    SH687.B373   1999
    799.1'757—dc21   98-20273
                                                CIP

ISBN 1-55821-705-3 (trade edition)
ISBN 1-55821-925-0 (limited edition)
ISBN 1-55821-926-9 (deluxe edition)

Rise free from care before the dawn, and seek adventures. Let noon find thee by other lakes, and night overtake thee every where at home. There are no larger fields than these, no worthier games may here be played.

—H. D. Thoreau, *Walden*

Crazy for Rivers

One

That autumn, I went a little crazy for rivers. The weather was unusually mild in northern California, where I live, and I had some time to spare and couldn't imagine a better way to spend it than in the high mountain country as the leaves began to fall. I fished the Merced and the Stanislaus, the Kings and the North Yuba, and I had some luck on them all and might have fished the Tuolumne, too, if nature hadn't dealt me a setback. It was a good period in my life, calm and reflective, even happy. The days flowed by unbroken, in perfect sunlight, and often I found myself thinking back over the years and thanking the heavens I'd come to be where I was, knee-deep in a trout stream with a fly rod in my hand.

Some people are born anglers, but I was not, even though my father had a passion for fishing. When I was a boy, I used to hear him complain about his distance from a decent lake as he dodged the traffic between our Long Island home and his office in Manhattan. He'd grown up in rural Michigan, the last of twelve children. His older brothers had taught him to love the outdoors, so he came by his longing honestly. His father—my grandfather, a stocky Slav always dressed for a wedding in a three-piece wool suit from Dubrovnik—was fond of the woods, as well, and saw no irony in decorating the tavern he owned with his cherished forest creatures (deer, moose, even hawks) stuffed and mounted.

For some reason, I'd met only a couple of my paternal uncles, so I enjoyed being told stories about them, especially about John, the eldest, who was a legendary hunter. He had shared a bed with my father for a while. That wasn't uncommon in large families in those days, and it might never have been mentioned at all, except that John talked and hunted in his sleep. In the middle of the night, he'd sit bolt upright in a trance, grab my father by the shoulders, shake him, and shout, "There's a bear in the room! Oh, no! He's going to attack us!" My father never saw the bear, of course, but it *seemed* real to him, and he would shiver and whimper until John

4

stuck out an arm like a rifle, took deliberate aim, and fired a fatal shot.

"Blam! Got 'im!" he'd cry. "We're *saved*!" Then he would roll over and go back to sleep.

Though I couldn't have known it then, not when I was still a child myself, I understood later that my father told such stories because he missed the folks on the Upper Peninsula and felt nostalgic for his youth and its sporting pursuits. His success in business had separated him from much that he cared about and had affection for, so every summer he would saddle up his family for a two-week vacation at a fishing resort, ordinarily in Minnesota—my mother was from there—but once in darkest Maine, at Sebago Lake, where I was puzzled and a bit frightened by the taciturn, stiff-spined, pipe-smoking men in flannel shirts, who were already cutting firewood in July.

I got my first fishing lessons on those trips, but I was a lackluster student. I could swing a Louisville Slugger with aplomb and even hit the long ball, but I was terribly awkward with a spin rod. Whenever I snarled my line or tossed a Jitter-bug into a tree, my father would become flustered, carrying on about the minutes he was losing as he untied the knots and retrieved the plugs from limbs. He had a temper back then and lacked the patience to be a sympathetic teacher. We hardly ever caught any fish, either, so my brother, David, and I, being enterprising lads, would amuse ourselves by liberating minnows from the minnow bucket, shooting at squirrels with a Whammo slingshot, and conducting stupid giggling fits whose sole purpose was to further annoy the old man.

The only rewarding fishing I ever had on vacation, in fact, was courtesy of Carl Peterson, my mother's father, who guided us kids around Paradise Lake in a rowboat, in 1956. Carl managed an apartment building in St. Paul and bought me my first official cowboy outfit—chaps, spurs, boots, the works. I liked him a lot, although not as much as I liked my Uncle Ned, a former star player in a semi-pro baseball league, who worked as a mailman and let me walk his route with him sometimes. Ned always had a powerful thirst, and if the weather happened to be humid, we would be forced to stop at a few saloons along the way, where my uncle would polish off a quick draft beer, often paid for by an admiring fan, while I thumped the pinball machine and developed bad habits at an early age.

Carl Peterson didn't fish much himself, but he had patience in his favor and knew that children in boats are most content when they have something to do. He let us fish for easy-to-catch crappies instead of the tricky bass or pike my father went after, and we hauled in so many of them so fast that we got our picture in the local paper holding up a stringer to show off our forty or fifty victims. It still astonishes me to see how proud I look, a sophisticated East Coast youth of thirteen with his hair styled in a fashionable "Hollywood" crew cut (flat on top and slicked back at the sides), secretly imagining his future as a rock-and-roll star, even as he poses with a bunch of dead crappies at Paradise Lake.

That fine adventure and our mini-aura of celebrity weren't enough to convert me, though. I really hated fishing by the time I turned sixteen. I rebelled against the entire concept of a family vacation and whined and protested until my parents agreed to let me stay home alone. (Not incidentally, that was the summer I lost my virginity to a lusty cheerleader in my very own upstairs bedroom, treating her to an ice-cream pop from a circling Good Humor truck immediately afterward because I had no idea what else to do.) I thought that sitting in a boat in the middle of nowhere was the dumbest activity known to mankind and swore I would never fish again—and I might have kept my promise, too, if my brother hadn't intervened by accident, thirteen years later.

I had taken Horace Greeley's advice by then and migrated west to seek my fortune, although not to *work* for it. I was living in San Francisco, in a spacious Haight-Ashbury Victorian that we renters failed to dust even once during our tenancy. My hair, suffice it to say, was not in a Hollywood crew cut anymore, and I'd mastered the fine art of slacking. As for David, he had what we referred to as a "straight" job (book salesman in Manhattan), but he'd managed to finagle a transfer to California so he could savor the hippie glories I'd described to him. On a whim, he brought some of my father's old tackle with him, and we passed a comical evening sorting through it, laughing as we dredged up the names of the long-forgotten lures—Hawaiian Wigglers in lurid purple skirts, an evil black Sonic, a wacky Crazy Crawler, and a single Lazy Ike, yellow with bright-red polka dots.

We stored the tackle in the basement, where it languished. It might have stayed there forever, or at least until our landlord evicted us, if I hadn't fallen for a new girlfriend and invited her on a romantic trip to the Sierra Nevada. Not that I'd ever been to the Sierra Nevada myself, but that hardly matters when you're wild about someone. I studied the maps and made the plans and knew in my heart that we would be all right wherever we landed, as long as the place had a bed. After packing the car and loading the cooler, I went downstairs at the last minute and grabbed one of the vintage spin rods and a reel, South Bend and Zebco respectively, although I wasn't truly conscious of why I might be doing it and moved about as a person does in a daze or a dream.

We wound up in a rustic cabin on Stuart Fork of the Trinity River, in the shadow of the Trinity Alps. The cabin resembled a packing crate inside and had an icebox instead of a fridge, but it fronted on the river and was blessed with an open-air porch, where we slept on a lumpy mattress and gazed up at the brilliant stars and moonlit peaks and felt that we must be the most fortunate couple on earth. We went hiking, played games of cribbage, and cooked steaks over the coals, and yet not once did it occur to me that I was reliving the family vacation. I was still very young then and blind to so many things, and I didn't realize how a past experience can touch us deeply, can shatter us or set us free, even though we've never reckoned with its power. But I know it now. The past is never wholly gone.

Those days in the mountains were glorious days. It was late in September, but the afternoons were still blazing hot, and we liked nothing better than a nap on the porch after lunch, with the sun falling all around us and the air rich with the scent of sun-warmed pines. One afternoon, I woke before my girlfriend and stood looking at the river, so low and clear I could count the pebbles of the streambed. Trout in there? I doubted it, but I rigged up the rod for fun, rolled up my jeans, and waded barefoot into the water. I could see the sun glinting off the spoon I'd bought at the resort's store and could hear some Steller's jays bickering in the tall trees, and I drifted so far away from Stuart Fork that when a fish hit my lure, it had the effect of yanking me out of the clouds and back into my body.

High up leaped a silvery little rainbow, as hooked in the moment as I was.

Two

So I became a fisherman by chance, through the loving seeds planted in me long ago, in childhood. The light, the water, the pines, even the sweet ease of an afternoon nap, they all added up to a treasured memory I'd blocked, and I knew that I was in the grip of something profound. For a time, I was obsessed with fishing and never passed up an opportunity to go exploring and wet a line. My life was still blissfully disorganized, with no direction or goals to get in the way, and I took full advantage of my idleness. I had an old car for transport, enough money for burgers and beer, and many free hours to roam, experiment, and daydream. Such is the idler's just reward.

I fished for catfish in the sloughs of the Sacramento River delta and trapped crawdads in the bargain, using a crab net and some cans of dog food for bait. I fished for stripers off the rocks in Sausalito and hooked rockfish instead (big surprise) and tried to cook up a bouillabaisse, only to find that my catch, when gutted, stank of diesel fuel. I fished for sturgeon in Richardson Bay with light spinning tackle (big mistake) and tied into a prehistoric monster that stripped my reel (the old Zebco again) in five seconds flat. I fished for black bass in the Russian River and ocean perch in the surf near Pacifica, but it was fishing for trout that truly captivated me and sent my spirits soaring.

I liked the wild, beautiful country where trout are often found, the solitude of walking along a river and being drawn more completely into the landscape, and how the sound of a fast-flowing stream could wash away my blues. I'd always had too much nervous energy to sit calmly on a bank and meditate on the natural world as enlightened monks are said to do, so I liked all the action, too, the wading and casting and stalking, my eyes open to creatures I had never noticed before, tiny midges on the wing, a belted kingfisher's swooping glide, seeing more than I could say in words and learning to trust my instincts.

Soon enough, I traded in my spin rod for a fly rod. It was a low-end fiberglass Fenwick, and when I first tested it at the casting pools in Golden Gate Park, I sensed in its suppleness and grace an artistry I might never fully master.

I took my new rod into the field right away, up to Downieville, a Gold Rush town in the Sierra Nevada foothills, on the North Yuba River. My girlfriend, still the same one, accompanied me; she would later become my wife. Diana fished indifferently when she fished at all, but she had a taste for the road and a tolerance for my moods and excesses, as well as an affection for the mountains that went back to her own childhood camping trips in the Colorado Rockies. She was happy with a good book and a comfortable chair to read it in, played a much better game of cribbage, and seemed not to care if I stayed on the stream until the light had faded, as I did almost every evening.

Downieville was still rough around the edges in those days, with a fair complement of rednecks, so for safety's sake I would tuck my long hair under my baseball cap whenever we strolled the plank sidewalks on Main Street. We jawed with the grizzled old prospectors who sold gold flakes and nuggets along the way, each prized specimen showcased in a glass vial. Lodging was at a premium, but we were lucky again and found a cattle ranch that rented out its musty bunkhouse for a reasonable price. The bunkhouse had seven bedrooms, and we christened them in honor of their imaginary occupants—Shorty, Curly, Tex, and Doc, we had our own set of wrangler dwarfs—and slept in a new room every night, drifting off to the distant clanging of cowbells in the dark pasture below.

There was harmony on the home front, but I met with chaos on the river. The North Yuba, a typical Sierra stream of pools, riffles, and pocket water, had me absolutely baffled. I flailed about and suffered wind-knots by the dozen, slipped and fell and banged up a knee. Though no insects were hatching, I insisted on fishing dry flies only (it was more fun), but they floated back toward me much too fast to handle. One morning, I watched in despair as an Adams skated past me at top speed, as if trying to escape. While my fingers were tangled in coils of line, I felt a tug behind me. In my confusion, I did what I *had* been doing and threw another cast upstream, but a trout fingerling had taken the Adams and went sailing by overhead. No one believes me, but I swear I saw the panic in its eyes.

I improved. I had to, or else I'd risk being arrested for streamside mayhem. I put in more practice time at the casting pools and read every book about trout fishing I could lay

16

my hands on, from such ancients as Dame Juliana Berners to modern gurus like A. J. McClane. My favorite instructor was Ray Bergman, whose classic *Trout* was originally published in 1938. I owned a copy of the second edition, already in its twelfth printing in 1973. The dust jacket was wonderfully expressionistic in the manner of Emil Nolde. A brook trout was chasing a mayfly through the air, over a body of water as stormy as the Atlantic Ocean at supreme high tide. There was no photo of Bergman, but I pictured him as the sort of gentle sage who sits outside a country store, whittling with his knife and never hurrying anywhere.

Bergman's book was full of quiet wisdom. The author came across as humble, knowing, and kind. He had real compassion for beginners and zeroed in on helpful practical matters. His was the voice of experience, that was certain, and I suspected he must once have made the same mistakes I was making. I thought that if he wandered along the North Yuba and stumbled upon me thrashing, he wouldn't embarrass me by offering any advice. Instead, he would lower his head, glance mercifully away, and whistle a merry folk tune, maybe "Jimmie Crack Corn" or "Big Rock Candy Mountain," while he skirted the area where I was doing the damage. Of his book, he wrote, "I hope we will become friends because of it."

Best of all, Bergman had a knack for conveying technical information in a simple way. When he discussed a river and how to fish it, I could see the boulders, holes, and oxbows, and I followed his every digression with keen attention. I didn't want to turn out like one of the dim-witted anglers he focused on in his object lessons, those callow men who were capable of working a run for hours without a single rise, doing everything wrong, dressed in red shirts and throwing shadows on the water, crashing through the brush like commandos, letting their barking dogs splash after beavers, and ignoring the most basic civilities—while wily old Ray observed them and recorded their foolish errors. And when they gave up at last and marched on to the next pool, snookered once again, Bergman would add insult to injury by fishing the same stretch with superb results.

I earned a payoff for my diligent studies, finally. This happened on the Bear River near Colfax, on a November afternoon toward the end of the season, with a chilly wind blowing and bruised-looking clouds bunched on the horizon. The Bear wasn't a pretty stream where I fished it, not at all. Murky and green, it tumbled down a spillway from an impoundment called Rollins Lake and rolled under an aged highway bridge that had ivy growing from the cracked concrete. Trash was frequently strewn about the river, fast-food wrappers, Styrofoam tubs that had once held night crawlers, empty pints of liquor—in short, the Bear summoned no thoughts of the sublime, but it had the singular merit of being relatively close to the city, less than a three-hour drive from my house.

To fish the Bear properly, you had to do some climbing over rocks and, if you ventured very far downstream, some bushwhacking through blackberry vines. But there was a wide, food-rich pool by the bridge, and I'd seen a few trophy trout come out of it, although bait-dunkers had caught them. I seldom saw anyone fishing flies, in fact. Those of us who did took a backseat to the locals, who arrived early and could stay late, anchoring themselves at the choice spots with six-packs in paper sacks. And two men were stationed at the good pool when I got there, of course, drowning worms just as I expected, both of them in T-shirts despite the frigid weather, so I put a hundred yards between us and worked a Pheasant Tail nymph through some fast water for about half an hour, with no success.

Then I did something unusual, at least for me. I went back to the pool and stood patiently on the bank, as Ray Bergman always did, and watched the men and prayed that the temperature would keep dropping until they got so cold they'd have to pack it in. It took an eternity, but they quit before twilight, shivering and complaining, and left the pool to me. Remembering my lessons, I rested the water and considered how to approach it. There was a slick along the far bank, hard by a deadfall oak, where I had seen several bold swirls. I figured that was the spot to probe. My intuition told me to go with an attractor pattern, so I tied on a Bivisible as gaudy as a butterfly. It rode high and mighty on the water, settling into a perfect drift on the third cast. I saw a boil and then a slashing take, and I was into my first big trout ever, a thick-bodied brown about eighteen inches long, all the more lovely to behold in the flurries of snow that started to fall.

Three

I kept that fish, I'm sorry to admit, and made an elegant meal of it, although not before I had snapped its picture about as often as most parents photograph their first-born child. When I contemplate the photos now, I wonder who that frozen, red-nosed fisherman is, posed by the stream with a black watch cap pulled down over his ears. If the fabled Paradise Lake "Portrait of Teen with Dead Crappies" suggests my adolescent attitude of dominion over nature, "Portrait of Long-Haired Man with Big Brown Trout" conveys an innocence all novice anglers have for a time and ultimately lose. Soon I'd be turning down my nose at such trashy streams as the Bear and setting my sights on the great rivers of the West, whether or not I was truly ready for them.

How much work I still had to do became clear when I traveled to Idaho Falls to visit a friend, who had started a new job up there. He had trout fever, too, so we drove north that weekend to Henrys Fork of the Snake River, as tough a spring creek as any I know. It wasn't long before we saw how overmatched we were. My frantic casting scared off the wildlife for miles around, but the veteran next to me had no trouble gently dropping his fly in front of fish that were feeding eighty feet away. His fifteen-foot leader was almost invisible, but my store-bought model, at half that length, slapped the water like a piece of rope. My friend and I could have been using Lazy Ikes, so little interest did our offerings generate.

If I failed to measure up to the challenge of Henrys Fork on my first visit, I still came away from Idaho in love with the landscape. That broad, open, seductive country, so different from the congested urban places where I'd always lived, spoke to my soul. I would have stayed on for another week or so if I could have, not even to fish but just to cruise the back roads in a borrowed truck and watch the flocks of Canada geese on the wing, honking in huge Vs across the sky, but I didn't have as much free time anymore. However belatedly, I'd set a goal for

24

myself and was trying to become a writer, probably because, as W. H. Auden once said, it *looks* easy; and I stuck to a rigorous schedule and labored to squeeze out a few paragraphs every day that wouldn't make me squirm in the morning.

But finally, after much struggle, I completed a manuscript I could face without remorse, and sometimes even with joy, and when the Viking Press published it in 1980, it brought me my first fishing partner, Bob Royer, an old friend I hadn't seen since we were Peace Corps volunteers in Nigeria some fifteen years before. Bob had read a nice review, bought the book and read it, and sent me a congratulatory letter in care of the publisher. He was too polite to say so, but I'm sure he found it hard to believe I'd really written it, because in West Africa I had produced only a modest folio of amateurish poems I would declaim, à la Dylan Thomas, in palm-wine bars with thatched roofs; while I was equally shocked to learn that Royer, who wasn't known for his diplomacy, had gone into politics and now claimed to be a deputy mayor in Seattle.

We arranged to meet soon after that at the San Francisco airport. Bob was flying home from some budgetary sessions in Washington, D.C., and planned to stop over for a night or two with my wife and me, so he and I could do some catching up. As I waited for his plane, I worried that I might not be able to pick him out of the crowd after such a long time, but there he was—and he looked awful! He was slump-shouldered, graying, a little seedy around the edges, and toting a bureaucrat's leather briefcase that was probably stuffed with unsavory classified documents from the CIA. How had he gotten so old, when I was still so young? I stepped cautiously forward to greet him, afraid I might shock him and cause a heart attack, but he walked right past my outstretched hand.

Seconds later, the real Bob Royer emerged from the plane. I'd had the wrong guy, as it turned out. The real Bob Royer carried a briefcase, too, but he had a bounce to his step and a grin I recognized, and he was not any grayer or seedier than I. He had indeed transformed himself into a politician and owned the parking tickets to prove it, over two hundred of them he'd collected while he was running his brother's successful campaign for mayor. It did me good to know that a certain degree of nepotism had figured in his rise to the top. I prepared myself for tales of smoke-filled rooms, but Bob went on instead about his current infatuation, which, by the sheerest coincidence, happened to be fly fishing.

Over some bourbon in my kitchen, we talked about the streams we had fished and those we still hoped to fish, and also about Nigeria, inevitably, recalling how Bob's cook, whose name was Felix, had once fixed us a special dinner of grilled porcupine and how after it we had toured the town's nightclubs and danced, fueling ourselves with Star Beer, a native brew potent enough to induce hallucinations; and how on late nights we would open my 1966 edition of the *World Almanac*, read the obituary list out loud, and pour libations on the floor to the honorable dead who deserved it, appropriating a Nigerian custom; and how it felt to teach in a mud-brick classroom in a subtropical rain forest with pesky goats and guinea fowl meandering in, while the students were discussing Jane Austen; and how the Oba of Benin City, who rode around in a shiny red convertible, would invite Royer to his walled compound to shoot games of eight ball on his imported pool table.

We talked about the good times and the bad ones, too, when the civil war started and we were forced to leave. We talked about the pain of that departure and all we'd left behind, and about the horrors that had rained down on our friends in that faraway country and how powerless we were in the face of it, halfway around the world. It was almost light when we quit talking at last and went to bed, but there were more (and happier) memories in the morning, so we agreed to continue our conversation on a fishing trip somewhere in the next few months.

I believe we chose the Rogue River in Oregon for winter-run steelhead, but I can't be certain. There have been lots of trips by now, and each blends into the next with a kind of symmetry that robs time of its meaning. For many years, it was a point of pride with us that even as we were dragged kicking and screaming toward our inescapable fate as responsible adults, we always managed to block out a few days to spend on a river; and those days are all linked in my mind now, joined in the way of postcards in fanfold pack.

We are on the Feather River in California, for instance, up near Mount Lassen, and as we're driving back to our cabin, we encounter a frantic (and unlikely) hitchhiker waving a filthy handkerchief. He's in his seventies, seriously unkempt, and apparently in flight from some mortal threat. A rattlesnake? A bear? He climbs into the backseat and mutters, "I know what *she* wants." He repeats the words again and again, varying the accent ("I *know* what she wants"), until it dawns on us that he has a lady friend stashed somewhere, and she's demanding more than another game of pinochle. The poor fellow is on the run from sex, but he seems to have nowhere to hide and gets out of the car exactly where we picked him up.

Or we're on the West Walker River, near Bridgeport, on a cold, stormy October afternoon. Our fingers are numb and our joints are stiff, so we decide to ditch the fishing and gamble at Lake Tahoe. We follow Highway 395, a route sometimes referred to as the "loneliest" in the state. There is no other traffic, of course. Hail pelts the car and blankets the windshield, and I can barely see and swerve to avoid hitting a boulder in the road. I keep right on going, but Royer insists we return and move the boulder to prevent somebody else from having an accident. I accuse him of leftover '60s idealism and remind him how *lonely* the highway is, but he nags, lectures, and ultimately prevails. He is later rewarded for being a Good Samaritan by winning big at roulette. I, on the other hand, am clearly a Bad Samaritan and can't cash a single bet all night.

Or we are on the Yakima River in Washington, where I catch a twenty-seven-inch rainbow as fat as a sow; or on the Firehole in Yellowstone, where a gangly moose tramps out of the woods and spooks us city boys into a sprint; or on Dry Falls Lake, a shadeless, treeless seep hole near Grand Coulee

Dam, where we cast chironomids to chunky trout suspended in clear water, as visible as bonefish in the Florida Keys; or on the Gallatin or the Madison, on the Skagit (no steelhead, plenty of rain), on Hat Creek and Hot Creek, on the Wenatchee (no steelhead again), on the Truckee (no fish, period); all very fine trips to be sure, and yet still merely an overture to the trip I suggested we make to Henrys Fork, as a way of getting even.

Four

*I*f Henrys Fork had me stymied on the first go-round, back in my novice days, I felt ready for it now. I was more experienced, wiser and cannier, almost skill-ful. When I laid out a cast, I didn't see people ducking any-more. I had dutifully studied my Ray Bergman, done some work in entomology, and even built up a small reference li-brary that I browsed through before any trip. Every volume I consulted had a mention of the celebrated stonefly hatch that takes place on the Snake and other major rivers of the West in the spring. There were enticing descriptions of the huge, juicy bugs falling from the sky in a blizzard, while the resident trout, waking from their winter doldrums, lost their usual caution, got greedy, and made mistakes. It sounded awfully good to me.

So in early May, just after the start of the season, Royer and I agreed to meet at the airport in Idaho Falls. Our destination was Harriman State Park, a sixteen-thousand-acre wildlife refuge tucked into the northeast corner of Idaho, close enough to Wyoming to be part of the Greater Yellowstone ecosystem. The land had originally belonged to several officials of the Oregon Shortline Railroad, who had purchased it with some fellow investors in 1902 and turned it into a cattle ranch. It had also served as a private retreat for wealthy families from the East, including the Guggenheims (copper barons), the Harrimans (railroad barons), and Charlie Jones, who ran the Richfield Oil Company.

For obvious reasons, Harriman State Park bore the nickname "Railroad Ranch." I'd walked some of it on my last visit and regaled Bob with tales of its glories. The Henrys Fork wound through it for about nine miles, crossing sage meadows, pastures, and marshes. There were two lakes, Silver and Golden, where trumpeter swans, the largest North American waterfowl, nested. I had seen ospreys and bald eagles and also sandhill cranes, who were hopping about and flapping their wings. The ranch was at an elevation of sixty-two hundred

34

feet and richly timbered with Douglas fir, lodgepole pine, and groves of quaking aspen. Deer and elk were common, while pronghorn and bison were sometimes sighted. If there was a prettier spot to go fishing, I had yet to discover it.

We reached the landmark of Last Chance, near the town of Island Park, that afternoon. The river ran parallel to the road, and I was amazed to find thirty or so anglers packed in shoulder to shoulder when Railroad Ranch was just a short hike away. I blamed it on the ever-diminishing spirit of American self-reliance, and on the lack of intrepid adventuring that the dozing suburbs had helped to foster. But no, I was wrong. When Bob got out and asked around, he learned the ranch had special regulations and wouldn't be open to anglers for a couple of weeks. It was my fault in the end. In my haste and excitement, I'd failed to read the fine print. That was a bad habit of mine.

Apologies done with, our choices were few and far between. We could join the gang at Last Chance, get in step with a conga line of nymphers by Box Canyon Campground, or drive on to Yellowstone. But I was fixated on the stonefly hatch at Henrys Fork and figured we ought to wait it out until morning, at least. Royer didn't protest. He was a friend, and there has to be a solid element of forgiveness in any friendship

35

for it to survive. Friends are recognized, not made, some wise person once said, and that rang true to me, as did another saying I'd copied into a notebook, stealing it from the composer Ned Rorem, who had it that friendship isn't about duration. It's about intensity.

We left Last Chance and checked into the cabin I'd reserved. Described as rustic in the brochure, it might have thrilled a group of pioneers who were sick of their Conestoga wagon, but it did little to elevate my mood. Not everything in it was broken—but almost. If you dared to sit in the single antique chair, you risked its collapsing in splinters. Still, the cabin was right on the Buffalo River, a turbid and, yes, *ugly* stream never to be featured in any photo essay on the purity of fly fishing, but we trudged down to it in the evening anyhow, fearing the worst. The Buffalo had soul, though, and compensated for its shabbiness by serving up eager brook trout who hit every fly we showed them with delirious, hell-bent abandon.

"Confidence builder," Bob said.

Last Chance was packed again in the morning. We didn't even bother with Box Canyon. Instead, we drove around in a funk and racked our brains for a solution. When we passed a Forest Service outpost, we stopped because it was there and chatted up a pretty young ranger at the information desk, raving about how far we'd traveled for this once-in-a-lifetime opportunity and relating our nearly suicidal despair on discovering that the park was still closed. Maybe it was our trustworthy aura, or maybe we were convincing liars, or maybe we looked as frantic as that old hitchhiker on the Feather River, because the ranger bit her lip and hastily scribbled a map that would lead us to a part of the river she and her boyfriend always fished. They always did well, too.

"He'll kill me if he finds out," she whispered, glancing over a shoulder. I took the oath and swore we would never tell, not while we were still in Idaho.

Her special hole was about ten minutes from the ranger station, at the base of a dam, where the Snake was very wide. A sign warned anglers to beware of rapid changes in the water level, but it had no effect on us, not so late in the game. If it had said DON'T WADE HERE OR YOU'LL DIE it might have given us pause, but anything less intimidating amounted to an idle threat. After all, a breeze was blowing, the sky was cloudy, and we could hear the suck of trout inhaling stoneflies. And we were the only ones around.

Stoneflies (Plecoptera) are bountiful insects, with almost four hundred species represented. They lay their eggs in fast-moving streams, and the exceptionally tiny nymphs molt several times before they're mature. The molting process lasts for a year, or for two years in some cases, particularly among the monster species who may have a body length of two inches and wingspan of four inches. When the stoneflies are ready to hatch, they crawl from the water to a rock or a tree trunk, shed their nymphal skin, let their wings and soft body parts harden, and take flight. In May and June, they swarm in immense numbers and provoke the sort of voracious feeding frenzy I'd read about.

Royer hustled into the water first and fished a bushy #6 Sofa Pillow he'd tied himself. Though I hate to admit it, he's a much better caster than I am, so it was a jealous pleasure to watch him tease a rising fish some thirty feet away, missing the drift he wanted on the first try and nailing it on the second. A hooked trout exploded into the air—and not just any trout, either, but a Snake River cutthroat, heavily spotted and seventeen inches from head to tail. He held up the fish to show it off. I doubt that he's felt like a genius very often in his life, but this was definitely one of those moments.

That afternoon provided the finest fishing I've ever had, bar none. The stoneflies kept hatching, hundreds of them, and we caught a trout every few casts, all substantial fish, with the longest taping out at better than twenty inches. The bushiest flies brought the hardest, fastest takes, so Bob tied hairier and hairier examples at streamside. They were as grotesque as creatures from a science-fiction movie.

"Hamburgers," he mused, a thread between his teeth. "These fish are hungry for hamburgers, that's what we'll give 'em."

We fished not until the light had failed but until we were sore-armed from casting and tired of catching trout. As we walked away from the river, I thought I must have crossed over into the realm of the eternally fortunate and would have such days forever after, but I was mistaken. It was only our turn to be rewarded.

At the cabin, Royer saw that he'd used almost all his red-squirrel tail on wings for his giant Sofa Pillows, so the next morning, first thing, we visited Will Godfrey's tackle shop. Henrys Fork at Last Chance was still jammed, and the store itself was full of disappointed fellows huddled over hot coffee and griping about their fishless fate. Probably we were glowing ourselves, or at least gloating, as we approached the counter. The man behind it (Will Godfrey himself, although we didn't know it yet) asked us how we were doing, and I was too pumped up to play it close to the chest and blurted out, "I've never caught so many big trout in my life."

That seemed to baffle Godfrey. He'd been hearing nothing but bellyaching lately. "Where are you fishing?"

Now I was the whisperer. "By the dam."

He gave us a funny smile and invited us into an office behind the counter. That's when we realized who he was. He riffled through some manila folders in a desk drawer, chose one, and passed us an eight-by-ten glossy whose gloss had mostly rubbed off. It had the look of a historical thing. Two young men, trim and fit, were sitting in a boat in the very same spot where we'd taken all our trout, just below the dam. Godfrey leaned forward and tapped one man with an index finger. "That's me," he said.

I squinted and compared and could see the resemblance. "Yes, it is."

He tapped the other man. "And that's Jack Hemingway. We used to fish there all the time."

Then Will Godfrey rocked back in his chair, as a man does after a gratifying meal, his hands folded over his belly, and told us some great fish stories, and I felt compelled to induct

40

myself into the clan of transitory geniuses that already included Bob Royer.

We didn't do as well on the river that day, of course, but it wasn't a bad day, not at all. After cleaning up, we treated ourselves to a terrific T-bone steak dinner at Phillips Lodge and phoned our wives to do the predictable boasting. We would have fired up cigars if any were available, but we had to make do with glasses of brandy at the table. And who should stroll in while we were celebrating? The pretty ranger who'd tipped us off. She had swapped her Smokey uniform for a flattering dress and held the hand of a low-browed, muscular kid—her boyfriend, we assumed. Her eyes brightened when she saw us, but she quickly dummied up and waltzed on by. I was tempted to shout hello and thank her, but I stuck to my oath and never said a word.

Five

*W*hen you're young and things are going well—and I *was* young on Henrys Fork that May, although I would have stubbornly argued the point—you think they'll go that way forever. There would always be an annual fishing trip, I told myself, imagining it would arrive in clockwork fashion, another kind of holiday, Thanksgiving or Easter in disguise, but I got ambushed by the demons of middle age, and some of my freedom slipped away. I seemed to have less time, too, and I complained about my distance from the water, just as my father had done. My life at forty-five, right on the money, felt constricted and compromised, and I had trouble staying inside my own skin.

A long, healthy marriage went untended and collapsed. Those innocent days on Stuart Fork belonged to another person.

It was not a happy period, obviously, and through it all I wondered if happiness, at least in its purest form—as a sort of buoyancy, even a state of grace—wasn't too much to ask for after a certain age. Yet life had surprised me so often in the past I couldn't truly believe in that theory, except during my worst moments of melancholy. It might be, though, that the happiness we stumble on when we're older is different in kind and has to arise unexpectedly, not from a desire satisfied or a goal achieved, or even from plain luck, but rather through a new understanding of some aspect of the world that had previously puzzled us. Happiness, then, as a solace or a freshening, an opening out.

I didn't see much of Bob Royer in the couple of years when I was adrift. He was sunk in his own misery and coping with his own set of problems. He had left politics and was struggling to define his future, puttering around the house while he considered his course of action. Once, he wrote me an entire letter about wanting to refinish a battered mahogany desk he'd salvaged from the junk heap, viewing its renovation in metaphorical terms; and I, ever the sympathetic pal, threatened to send him a cardigan sweater, a ream of sandpaper, and subscription to *Reader's Digest*. Another joke was that he ought to apply for a job advertised on Orcas Island, in the San Juans—that of a fish-hatchery manager. He did not, but we both still keep the ad on file, just in case.

In time, Bob's gloom lifted, as mine did, and he got back on his feet and developed a thriving consulting and public relations firm in Seattle; and in the autumn of the most recent El Niño, in 1997, we began talking about fishing together again.

El Niño was a media darling that season, covered widely on the West Coast. The name refers to a huge pool of curiously warm water that collects in the Pacific Ocean at random intervals and wreaks havoc with our global weather patterns. The last El Niño, in 1982, had done $14 billion in damages, while the one that was threatening us that autumn looked every bit as bad. It had already caused forest fires in the Amazon and a drought in Indonesia, so there was, in my neck of the woods, a mild but palpable dread. We were in for torrential rains, the forecasters said, but none of them dared to predict when the storms would actually start.

I bought into the black visions myself, of course, and began staring at every passing cloud with a severe sense of urgency. The pathetic fallacy grabbed hold of me next, and I pictured

47

El Niño as a malevolent cosmic being. In my paranoia, I was certain El Niño had targeted me in particular for destruction, so I took care of the household repairs I'd postponed for years, patching the roof on my leaky cottage and building a retaining wall to keep my front yard from sliding into the street. I replaced a section of rotted redwood fence and laid in a cord of oak firewood, too, ripping through two thousand dollars as fast as I ever had.

By the middle of September, I was sawing faulty limbs off my cherry laurel and hacking at the ivy, marching myself around like a mean-tempered straw boss. I might have carried on that way for months, but one afternoon, as I was pulling up some dying tomato plants, I got to contemplating their brief lives on earth and remembering how much delight they'd given me—tiny heirloom tomatoes bursting with flavor— and it made me aware of the fleetingness of all things. I thought about the time behind me, some of it wasted and some not, and about the time still ahead. If El Niño was going to wash away my meager domain, so be it—I said that out loud. Autumn was almost here, and I wanted to be on a river in the mountains, sooner rather than later.

So I phoned Royer and was cheered to discover that he was also sick of his routine. Bored and overworked, he told me

48

he'd go anywhere at all, no matter how good or bad the fishing might be. It would be enough, he said, to be gone from his office and sitting on a porch in the country, drinking a beer and eating a pound of bacon. He could have been sounding an anthem, I thought, for the weary middle years. He left the logistics to me, and that was bold of him after my performance at Railroad Ranch. But age had taught me to avoid making the same mistake twice (although I didn't always succeed), so I rose to the challenge and mapped out a trip that appeared to meet our criteria.

In a fly-fishing magazine, I came across an article about the Middle Fork of the Tuolumne River, where it flows through Stanislaus National Forest in the foothills above the Central Valley. In seductive images, the writer described the stream, deep in a canyon and a bit difficult to reach, but the trout were reported to be plentiful and mostly wild. The Tuolumne wouldn't offer us the big-league thrills we might have had in Trout Heaven, up in Idaho, Montana, or Wyoming, but it was fairly close to San Francisco, and we would save a bundle on plane fare. The magazine provided a list of accommodations close to the river. I booked us a small house at Pine Mountain Lake in Groveland, and we were on our way.

Six

*T*here is a rich expectancy in the act of packing for a fishing trip. Some people spend the last hours in a military fervor, with their gear in neat piles and a checklist in hand, as exacting as Douglas MacArthur on the eve of a campaign, but I tend to be cavalier and abide by a single rule: I make sure to pack my rod and reel. Basic, yes, but if you've ever arrived at a distant river without them, you'll understand. My father, on the other hand, was always overly prepared, his tackle box so heavy he could barely lift it; and yet at the lake, he'd meet a local Joe with some site-specific lure guaranteed to do the trick and would soon own a large assortment of this new model in various shapes, colors, and sizes, usually to no good purpose.

On the morning of our departure, Royer pulled up at my house in a nifty bottom-of-the-line Neon he'd rented at the airport. As I loaded the trunk, breathing in the new-car smell and its purely American air of promise, I felt a familiar upsurge of joy. No other nationality loves the road as much as we do, or believes so strongly in its transformative power. *See the USA in Your Chevrolet*, as the copywriters used to put it, cleverly suggesting that you need to be on four wheels to grasp the essence of our country. Dreams of glory invade us at the start of a long drive, and in our innocence we imagine all the pleasures about to accrue to us, while we repress any memory of flat tires, busted fan belts, or wailing children in need of a bathroom.

It was a warm Sunday toward the end of September when we set out, and the sky was cloudless and omenless. Soon we were beyond the suburbs of Livermore and moving into the farm country past Tracy. I had the impression that a camera lens was opening before my eyes to deliver more space and light, even more of the world. The highway steered us through Manteca, where there were produce stands galore, all displaying the last of summer's bounty and offering up a fragrance as ripe and heady as the very scent of desire; so we stocked up on peaches, plums, beefsteak tomatoes, some ears of white corn, and two slices of watermelon we ate on the spot, fruit so icy and sweet it made our teeth ache.

We traveled on through rolling hills, where the grasses were as dry as tinder and the color of wheat. Bob popped a cassette into the tape deck, and the car echoed with the rhythmic dance music of King Sunny Ade, transporting us back to Nigeria. What a fine planet this is, I thought. Here we are motoring through the San Joaquin Valley and listening to juju high-life music, while the sun roars down on us and turns California into Kansas. Next, Bob played a favorite (and appropriate) tape of his, one that featured Carl Sandburg reading his poems—a better choice, frankly, than his Vachel Lindsay tape. Friendship involves forgiveness, et cetera, so I tuned in to old Carl's strophes. His voice had a surprising bite to it, and I forgave him the bangs that always fell across his forehead in artful disarray.

> *They have yarns*
> *Of a skyscraper so tall they had to put hinges*
> *On the top two stories so to let the moon go by,*
> *Of one corn crop in Missouri when the roots*
> *Went so deep and drew off so much water*

The Mississippi riverbed that year was dry,
Of pancakes so thin they only had one side . . .

The road took an abrupt swing upward by Don Pedro Reservoir. We ascended from the Kansas prairie and went over a steep mountain that had been scorched in a fire, blackened and burned down to raw earth. There were a series of quick switchbacks and hairpin turns that afforded some daunting views into a bottomless chasm stacked with dead trees. Royer, in the passenger seat, looked extremely uncomfortable. He thrashed, fidgeted, and glanced the other way, punctuating his gyrations with a strange yipping noise, until we descended into the Stanislaus National Forest and reached Groveland, an old mining town, in the early afternoon.

After a lunch of pork ribs and tri-tip at a barbecue joint, we paid the obligatory visit to a local fly shop. The lonely clerk appeared to be put out by the sight of potential customers, but he freed himself from his chair after a while and assured us that the Middle Fork was in excellent shape. When I asked him how far away the river was, he yawned, scratched himself, and said, "It's about fifteen minutes from here to the road into the canyon."

"How long from there to the Tuolumne?"

"Another hour."

"That can't be," I said. "The canyon road's just five miles long on my map."

"You got a four-wheel drive?"

"No, a Neon," I told him, wishing I'd lied and said, "Yeah, dude, a Bronco."

"Well, you'll probably make it, anyhow." Here was the first sign that something might be wrong.

We moved into the house at Pine Mountain Lake and sorted through our tackle, eager to be on the river for the evening rise. I had fished the Tuolumne once on my own, in Yosemite, where it flows through alpine meadows at around nine thousand feet. It's no bigger than a brook in the park, but it soon takes a radical dip and drops about five thousand feet in just a few miles, emptying into Hetch Hetchy Reservoir. The stretch between the meadow and the reservoir is supposedly fishable, too, but I think you'd need a machete and a set of pitons. From Hetch Hetchy, the Tuolumne continues drifting downhill into the valley until it finally joins the San Joaquin River, near Modesto.

The afternoon was still quite warm when we left the house, with the temperature in the eighties. We found the canyon road without any trouble—fifteen minutes on the highway, just as the clerk had predicted. The road was a ribbon of cement-hard dirt, rutted, potholed, and rough on the tires. For a time, it passed through some forest land, and the trees obscured any chance of a view. Bob was handling the wheel, and he inched forward cautiously, yipping as he'd done on the burned mountain. He seemed really miserable, but he pressed on, anyway, one foot riding the brake and the other applying a butterfly kiss to the gas pedal until we rounded a bend and the trees fell away, and we were confronted by an astounding panorama of the canyon.

And not just any canyon, mind you. No, we were staring into the *Grand* Canyon of the Tuolumne, a fact that my angling-magazine writer had failed to mention. The sun, molten orange, was low in the sky, and it cooked the rocks and soil down below to a fiery mineral incandescence. The canyon was a magnificent pit, an utter miracle of geology, and way at the bottom, glittering like the tiniest speck of water, was the Middle Fork. An hour away? It would take us to six hours at the rate Royer was going. He was sweating now, as well, and his face was pale, drained of all blood.

His yipping got much louder as the road began to narrow. In another few minutes, it was scarcely wide enough to accommodate a single car, much less two. If anybody came driving up from below—*if* anybody had ever survived the drive down—Royer would be forced to park in a turnout, probably on the left side of the road, where the cliffs were sheer and the phrase "margin for error" had no meaning whatsoever. In the end, it was too much for him. He set the emergency brake, bolted, and jumped from the Neon.

"You drive," he said, breathing hard.

So I replaced him. What else could I do? When you've known a man for thirty years, you figure that you're aware of his phobias, but we're a mystery to one another, finally. I certainly never knew that heights bothered Bob, any more than he knew how much I hated to be in a movie theater unless I had an aisle seat, so I could escape in an instant from a rotten film. I released the brake and crawled forward for another hundred yards, but he was so trembly and sweaty I started seeing the canyon the way he did, as a fierce, all-devouring death trap. I caught his phobia like the flu and almost yipped myself, imagining how one small miscue could pitch us over the rim.

"You want to turn around?" I asked him.

"Might not be a bad idea," he said.

There it was, the understatement of the decade.

We passed the waning hours in a bizarre search for a less

dangerous route to the stream, first entering Yosemite at Big Oak Flat and proceeding on to Hetch Hetchy—acres of concrete, no access there—and then trying a paved road out of Groveland that wound downhill at a reasonable tilt. It did conk out right at the Tuolumne, but the river was foaming with whitecaps and so big that we'd need a boat to fish it. The sky was almost dark, too, so we reluctantly surrendered, although not before we chatted with the only other fool hunkered there in the depths.

He was a stringy-haired guy in mangled clothes, who'd been sleeping in his truck for the past few days. He came from Vallejo, in the East Bay. His worms had died on the hot drive through the San Joaquin, he told us, mourning them a little, but he still planned to go fishing. He slipped on a knapsack, fired up a Camel, and grabbed a spin rod in one hand and a metal detector in the other. The odds that he was also packing a handgun were extremely high. Woe be it to any backwoods Tuolumne troll that crosses this guerrilla's path, I thought.

"I guess I got about thirty minutes of daylight left," he said with an optimistic grin, sallying forth into the pitch-black canyon. We stood there and watched him in wonder until he blended into the night and disappeared.

Seven

*I*n the morning, feeling sheepish, Royer and I regrouped. Our failure didn't sit well with us, not at all, and I wondered if we could possibly be the same bold fellows who used to roam the African bush without the slightest worry, unafraid of the poisonous snakes (deadly green mambas), the scorpions, the carpenter ants, and the Caedes mosquitos whose sting gives you dengue fever. Nothing seemed lethal to us back then, nothing threatened. Youth is truly squandered on the young, I thought. I saw my future at that moment as a mass of incipient phobias about to swallow me whole.

With the aid of maps, an atlas, and several buckets of hot

coffee, we managed to devise an alternate plan. I'd paid the rent on the house in advance, so we were committed to another night there, and decided our best bet would be to try the Merced River in Yosemite, although it would require a lot of travel time. The summer high season was over, and the park wouldn't be crawling with tourists, plus the Merced was right off the road. Perfect for old men, really.

I was in a nasty mood, all right, but the fates soon showed me how much worse things *could* have been for us. At a store in Buck Meadows, where we bought some bread, cheese, and beer for a streamside lunch, the cowboy working the cash register was in terrible shape. He had a big silver rodeo buckle on his belt and moved as stiffly as somebody who has fallen down a flight of stairs. He was black-and-blue everywhere—forehead, eyes, nose, knuckles, ears, and even cheeks, with a slash of dried blood in his mustache for good measure. Either an ornery bronc had thrown him, or he'd had the misfortune to walk through the wrong set of swinging saloon doors.

"Morning," Royer said cheerfully, pretending not to notice. "How you doing today?"

"Bad," the cowboy replied.

End of conversation.

As we cruised away from Buck Meadows into wilder territory, I felt myself filling up again with the oxygen of blind faith. I was experiencing the same rush of adrenaline that sends a man marching into a canyon with a metal detector after dark, I suppose, but I was unable to control the sensation. The prospect of another river—any river, it seems—causes my blood to percolate and my hopes to inflate. I always imagine a stream that's waiting to welcome me, all ambrosia, all elegant casts and instant hookups—and so it was for once on the Merced, although we were deceived at first.

We were a mile from the park gate when, itchy to start, we paused to inspect the river. From the road, it looked to be nothing more than a few slicks of water in a field of monumental boulders. I had the distinct impression that a hot summer sun had been beating on the Merced for months and had reduced it to a trickle. But when Bob scouted the stream up close, he saw that the slicks were actually deep pools. The boulders served as a kind of camouflage. They were so immense they dwarfed everything else around. We caught some trout right off the bat, using a variety of nymphs—Hare's Ears, Gold Bead Princes, Zug Bugs. The light was intense and revealing, and we had to sneak up to the pools and make short, accurate casts. The fish were just smallish rainbows, but we were glad to have them, anyhow, especially after our experience on (or off) the Tuolumne.

Around noon, we quit and had some lunch. I sat by the stream and relaxed, my cap over one knee and a hand massaging my matted hair. Royer sliced off chunks of pepper Jack, while I got two ice-cold beers from the cooler, remembering another of my father's stories about growing up in Michigan and how he and his family would hike into the woods for picnics and feast on Cornish pasties, a favorite of the copper and iron miners on the Upper Peninsula—root vegetables and a little meat baked in a crescent-shaped pie that could be stuffed in a worker's pocket. As the youngest child, he had the job of sinking bottles of beer into the river (he never told me its name) at strategic points, so that his brothers wouldn't go thirsty while they were fishing.

As it happened, I had visited my father earlier that year, back in June, right after his eighty-fourth birthday. He still lives in the same Long Island house where I collected baseball cards and Elvis Presley records. He doesn't get around very well anymore, so we kept mostly to his small den. We talked or read or watched the races from Belmont, but one breezy, bell-clear morning he asked me to drive him to Captree

Beach. He wanted to look at the party boats there. He used to go out on them with a neighbor in the old days, fishing for fluke and flounder and always bringing along some sandwiches of Limburger cheese and onion—he could get away with those at sea. In the harbor, we sat on a bench, and he studied the waves, the sky, and the wheeling gulls until it got chilly, and he was ready to go home.

Royer and I fished the Merced again after lunch and then made a brief tour of Yosemite, gaping with the other human midgets at Half Dome, Cathedral Spires, and Bridalveil Falls. The next day, for a change of scenery, we moved on to the Stanislaus River near Strawberry, following Highway 108 into the Gold Country. The Stanislaus isn't a magnificent stream by any means, running as it does through a badly logged-over forest, but in autumn, with the temperature in the Sierra dropping rapidly, I thought it might yield up some decent fish. We had no luck through the afternoon and evening, though, despite a complex hatch of caddisflies, mosquitos, and gnats.

At dawn, we took our parting shot. We tramped down to the stream through a meadow, listening with distress to the crunch of frost beneath our feet. The weather had turned wintry overnight and demanded neoprene waders, down vests, and maybe even some mittens, but we didn't have so much as a heavy jacket between us. Stepping into the Stanislaus was a form of torture. The frigid water poured into our boots and drenched our socks, and I clenched my teeth to keep from screaming. It didn't warm up a single degree until the sun crested the trees. Then the air came alive with bugs again, as it had the evening before.

But I noticed an odd phenomenon this time—a single mayfly fluttering in regal fashion amid the other insects. A few minutes later, I saw a second mayfly, another solo pilot, so I tied on the only close imitation I had with me, thinking that a fish, like a person, might throw caution to the wind and snatch at something unique and possibly prized. Sure enough, I had a strike on my first cast and reeled in a sorry little four-inch rainbow, who had the bad manners to tear up my fly. I fluffed the feathers and dabbed the body with flotant, then cast to an undercut bank, where a grandfather trout burst up from the river to inhale it. Down he went, under the bank and into the weeds, tugging me toward the tangled depths and snapping off my leader.

I howled as if I'd been hooked myself and stalked out of the river. When I was done talking to the clouds, I waded back in and fished some other flies to match the hatch—an elk-hair caddis, a mosquito, a midge—but they didn't provoke a reaction. Bob was faring no better. He admitted to being awfully cold and wondered aloud if he still had any toes left. To check on them, he took off his boots and socks, dumped out the gravel, and showed me some startlingly pink appendages. That was all the evidence we needed to decide it was time to give up. We bid farewell to the Stanislaus and ate a hearty breakfast (eggs, home fries, toast, almost a pound of bacon), and afterward, with no regrets, we hit the road for home.

Eight

*I*n early October, in the little Marin County town where I live, just over the Golden Gate Bridge, I saw some deer moving along a game trail on a hillside near my house. The Japanese maples in my yard were touched with a first splash of crimson, another sure sign of autumn, but the evenings were still too warm to burn a fire. Waiting for El Niño to deal us a mortal blow, I dreamed I heard rain thundering in the night sometimes, only to wake in the morning to more of that perfect sunlight. Though I had a desk piled with papers, I couldn't resist the keen bite of temptation. In such glorious weather, didn't I owe it to myself to squeeze in another last trip to the high country before snow covered the mountains?

Let me admit it—I was crazy for rivers. The Merced, the Stanislaus, they were haunting me now, along with all the other streams I had fished down the years, a braid of water held tightly in memory, coil upon coil. But where to try next? I settled on a new river, the Kings in Kings Canyon National Park, failing to take note of the word "canyon" or consider the effect *any* canyon might have on my battered psyche. The route to the park led me into the Central Valley again, where the cotton fields were in bloom, their fluffy bolls in stark contrast to the parched earth. Dust blew up behind tractors, the heat was scorching, and the shady, green orange groves east of Fresno looked as inviting as an oasis in the desert.

But soon I was climbing into the Sierra Nevada, up to the park entrance at about eight thousand feet. A ranger gave me some maps and brochures and informed me that it was another thirty miles or so to Cedar Grove, where I could camp on the river. "You'll enjoy the drive," she said brightly. "It's so scenic!" In minutes, I saw what she meant and rejoiced that Bob Royer was safe in his office in Seattle. Kings Canyon was a massive stretch of glaciated terrain, so vast that the Grand Canyon of the Tuolumne would fit into its back pocket. It was literally breathtaking. There were people transfixed at every turnout, as if in the presence of something sacred. I recalled

74

how my Nigerian friends used to express their appreciation at such moments, snapping their fingers for emphasis and saying, "Wonderful!" as in *We are full of wonder!*

Slowly, slowly, I negotiated the road. "Wonderful!" I kept saying, as a sort of prayerful litany. "Wonderful!" The only desire in my body was to make it to Cedar Grove, and when I did I set up camp beneath the swelling granite formations of Grand Sentinel and North Dome, ancient rocks snoring through the centuries, and ate a cold supper of tunafish and crackers. By lantern light, I wrote in my notebook:

Kings Canyon, yikes! Felt like an explorer as I inched along in Old Paint. Never seen anything like this chasm, wild in a way Yosemite once was, a hundred years ago. Will I ever get out? Already planning strategies to rely on if the Toyota overheats, yet how good it feels to be here. This is nature, brother. This is look-over-your-shoulder-every-cast nature, until you get used to it and understand you and the bears belong here together.

Set up my tent around four, by the road's end. Nothing beyond here but more granite and explosive tectonics and the trails the Monaches walked in summer to trade with the Paiutes in Owens Valley on the other side, up over Kearsarge Pass (11,823') to barter acorn meal, deerskins, and arrow shafts made of tule reeds for Paiute pine nuts, salt, and obsidian for arrowheads.

75

Too beat this evening for a major expedition, plus I was a lit-
tle anxious about the bears (Uncle John, remember him?), so I
fished an easy run of the Kings next to the only motel in this part
of the park. Nobody else on the water. I tried big Stimulators,
sixes through tens, and caught three small trout in five casts, all
brookies, stout and boldly colored. Twice I broke off on larger fish
by striking too hard. Had a tense minute or two when I heard
some heavy padding in the forest, but it was just a geriatric buck
with a trophy set of antlers. He'd seen enough human beings in
his long life to totally ignore me.

I had read in a guidebook once that fly fishers frequently
catch twenty to twenty-five trout on the South Fork Kings
from the late afternoon through the evening, and I believe it
now. The famed October caddis were hatching in bunches, so
my Stimulators were an excellent choice. I did well at all
hours, except in the early morning when the ground was lay-
ered with frost. I fished on the fringes of stunning meadows,
where the willows had already turned gold and the sedges
were a russet color, with a few yellow corn lilies scattered in
the grass. On the high mountain ridges, the aspens were like
tongues of flame leaping out from a dark green tier of pines
and firs. I could have stayed in the park forever.

After three days, those papers on my desk reached out and

grabbed me by the throat, though. It's time to go to work, they said, you're having too much fun—and yet I couldn't stop myself! On the way back, I made a detour to fish the Kings River outside Fresno, below Pine Flat Lake. The area was so close to the urban core I had to step over empty Colonel Sanders buckets to get to the water. There was something fruitless about the escapade, but it didn't hit me with full force until I started casting a Stimulator along the fender of a red Mustang convertible sunk in the stream. In the interest of anthropology, I asked about it and learned that some Fresno folks wash their cars in the Kings. The Mustang had just slipped its brake and gone for a swim.

Home once more, I put away my gear for the season, hung my waders from a nail in the basement, and stowed my good rod in its proper case; and two weeks later, in early November, when the rains still had not begun, I retrieved it all, laid in a fresh supply of flies, and headed for Downieville, that foothill town out of my past, a past that's never wholly gone. In the sharp-edged autumn light, the frame houses on Main Street, sturdy and white, evoked an atmosphere of New England. No geezers were selling nuggets on the plank sidewalks anymore, but I watched a caravan of mountain bikers whistle through like a vision of the future, drawn as if by a magnet to a bakery sign that advertised ESPRESSO, CAFÉ LATTE, and CAPPUCCINO, the pleasures of the city spreading far afield.

If my musty old bunkhouse was still for rent, I couldn't find a listing for it in the phone book. Instead, I checked into a motel on the North Yuba, where the Downie River, a small, riffly stream, flowed into it. I could hear both rivers when I lay in bed, and I fell asleep to the sound of them and slept hard and well. The mountain mornings were very cold now, so I drank strong tea and read or wrote in my room until the air warmed up, around nine o'clock. Sometimes there were splinters of ice on the parking-lot puddles when I set off. I fished every day straight through until dark, feeding myself from a knapsack, eating an apple or a pear or some cheese and bread whenever I got hungry.

I drove far back into the forest to fish Lavezzola Creek, known for its wild fish, but it was thin and spotty so late in the year. I fished Pauley Creek in town, too, and caught a nice brown. Up in Sierra City, I fished the North Yuba where Haypress Creek enters it. The river was low, so I was able to work the pools by hopping from stone to stone. I waded in sneakers and jeans with the sun on my face, hearing the buzz of chain saws and the tick of leaves on the water. The leaves fell steadily in a shower of yellow and gold, skittering about in a breeze,

78

and I sat on a boulder and watched them for a long time until somebody in a camper interrupted me, shouting from a bridge above, "Doing any good?"

"I'm doing great!" I shouted back, but the honest answer was that fishing had fled from my mind entirely. Alert again, I hopped to the next pool and tied on a fancy caddis emerger. A trout rose up at once to take it. It was another brown, only twelve inches long but very fat—a pound or so, I'd guess—and dappled with reddish spots. The burnished gold of its belly echoed the falling leaves. As I released it, I recalled the many photos of me posing with fish (Paradise Lake, the Bear River) and imagined a day might come when I could sit by a stream without fishing at all, just meditating as the monks were said to do, although I didn't believe I'd ever be enlightened.

That night, I stayed up late. I wrote in my notebook and heard the sound of the rivers, and when I was finished writing I opened a bottle of red wine, feeling blessed by the same sort of luck I'd had in Downieville so long ago, back when I was a novice and the world still looked shiny in every corner. I thought about the friends, lovers, and family I had fished with, where they were now and what they might be doing, and I thought about my father especially and our summer vacations in Minnesota when I was a child and had such certainty about life, before I knew anything about letting go. It must all be catch-and-release in the end, I thought, all part of a flow whose essence we can never truly grasp.

I had planned to fish the Downie River on my last morning in Downieville, but I didn't. Finally, I'd had enough. I was through with trout fishing for the season—really. As I left town, the leaves were still falling in a torrent, whipped about in a growing wind, and they were falling on my street when I got home. El Niño delivered its first big storm a few days later, a whopper that rolled in from the Pacific, dumped a foot of snow in the Sierra Nevada, and had the skiers dusting off their skis. I built a roaring fire in my fireplace and listened to the rain pounding on my patched roof with a deep sense of satisfaction. Maybe I was ready for a harsh winter. I had my solace, an autumn filled with rivers.